What Weeds Are Thinking

Written by Erica Crockett

Illustrated by Sarah Ragan Olson

Corvid Tear Media

Printed in the United States of America

ISBN 978-1-942300-06-9

First Printing, 2018

Layout design by Jenny Flint

Published by Corvid Tear Media
Boise, Idaho
www.corvidtearmedia.com

For all the weeds murdered for millenia:

R.I.P.

Redroot Pigweed

"I taste just like bacon.

Also, it's Opposite Day."

COMFREY

"What do you mean this isn't dirt surrounding my roots?

You spread this thick, odorous muck up to my main stem and expect me to just *wallow* in it after I find out it's manure?

Why don't you call it what it is, huh?

Cow feces.

You're tucking me into shit that comes from the prolapsed anuses of bovine and telling me to get over it? Screw your nutrient content. I can get my nitrogen fix the way nature intended!

Via the decaying corpses of my relations."

Thistle

"Look, there is a very easy way to remember the proper usage of the words *homely* and *comely*.

When one is homely, one is so strikingly ugly they are better suited to life spent in the home, you see, away from windows. A shut-in, if you'd like.

Where as one who is comely is super tight (if a body is had) and lickable (if a tongue is had) and darn pretty. So much so, one like this has the tendency to come a lot (if come is had). Comely, accounting for the staggering amounts of orgasms they have while sexing other comely creatures.

I hope this clears up any confusion. Oh, now I've stymied you over the origins of my book learning, have I? I tire of you. Put your fingers on my spiny, purple bits and squeeze."

DANDELION

"Blow off my noggin with your stank breath when I'm old and gray? Or rip my nubile, sunny dome from my thin frame in callous disgust? Bud, I ain't no dandy fluff. There's a reason the French named my kind *lion's tooth*.

Come any closer with those meat appendages and I'll sever your skull with the power of botanical telekinesis. Use its red liquid on my leaves like you use the pollen of my peeps on your skin to what, mimic incontinence? Scream out, *Eww! Pee!?*

I'll have you holler in terror instead. Right before I pop your fleshy cranium off that gangly waddle body. Rub it down the line of my leaves. Scream out, *Eww! Blood of a Motherfucker!"*

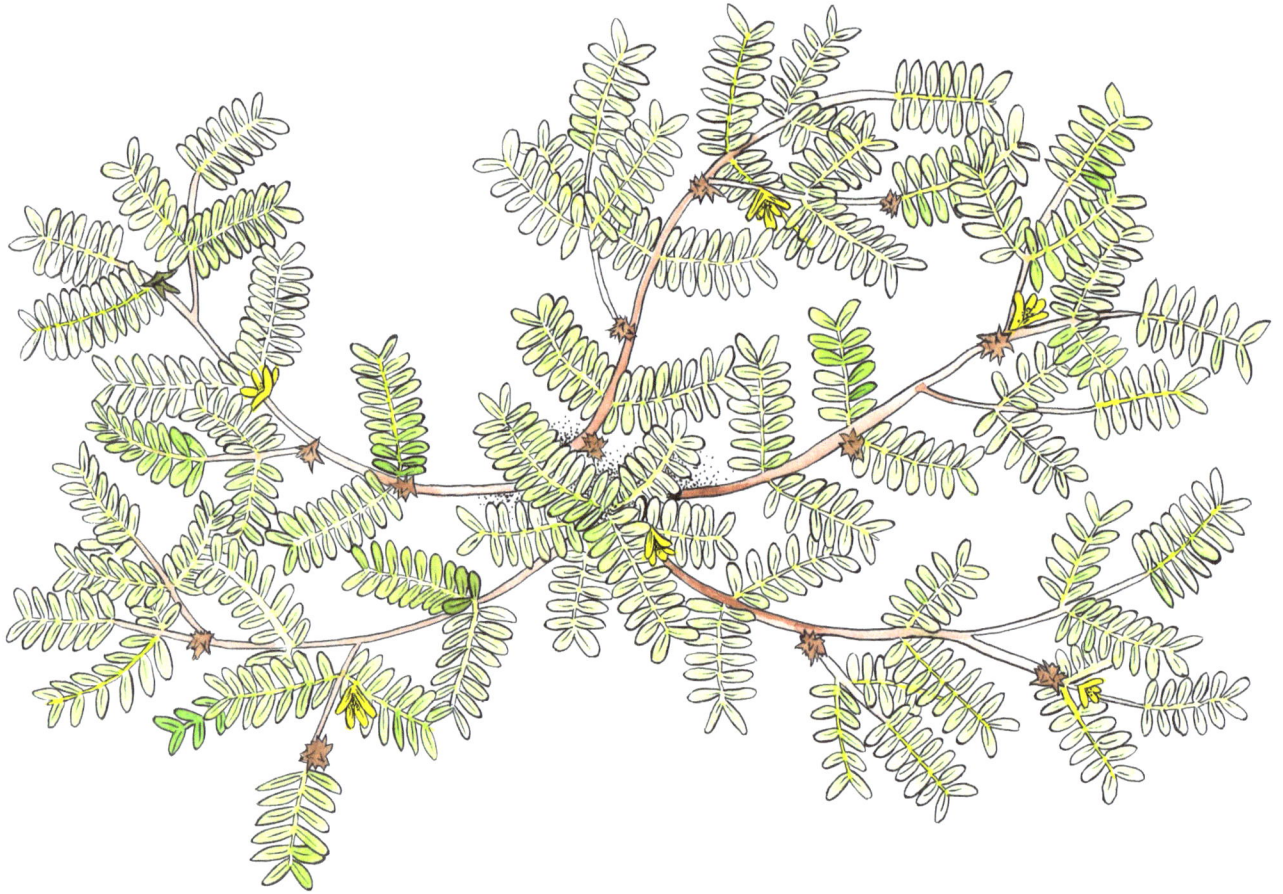

Goatheads

"What do I always says? I tells them $50 for the first poke and $35 for each poke after.

But do they give me dough? Nah, they moan about the power of my pokes. Leaves them deflated or bloody.

But I don't enter rubber or flesh for free. No sir.

When they don't pay, I retaliate.

With more poking.

I'm beginning to see a hole in my plan."

Clover

"Last spring, a seventeen-year-old Coachella attendee with a bull ring nose piercing and liquid eyeliner mistook our airy fluffs for vegan, non-GMO, red-kernel corn puffs while high on bath salts. She decimated an entire field of us while mumbling about her look being really choice for Instagram marketing."

We could see she was selling nothing more than naïve youth and butt cheeks round as the full moon that hangs over our land.

It's because of us she experienced dystonia, her body contorting into a mess of sharp angles at every joint and freezing in place while she was on the ground. She lived long enough to snap a selfie, her duck lips coated in herbaceous dander. Granted, it was likely the bath salts that killed her, but we like to think we did our part.

You're welcome."

Morning Glory

"No, I'm not high.

Why? Do I look it? Because that's not, like, my natural state. You guys can say, man, doing datura is like doing LSD but to be fair, I was around long before your little stamps and dropper bottles.

My cell walls aren't juiced. Just twining my little graspy tendrils around this here chain link fence. Boring stuff. Pulling water from the dirt down below. Catching some sunrays to quell the munchies.

NO. I said I wasn't high, dude. GTFO if you're gonna be accusing me.

Just, if you do leave, watch out for the maroon, nine-eyed dancing jalapeño behind you. He looks spicy."

MILKWEED

"You like monarch butterflies, you giant butt-
holes? Their orange and black flutter bits
make you pop boners when one lands on your
shoulder or flies by your nose? Those gentle
and majestic creatures riding on zephyrs and
sprinkling babies with fairy luck, reminding
you of love and hope and other pussy-ass
shit? You *lurve* them?

Well their larva pups eat on me and I don't
mind. Tickles, but no biggie. They hang their
chrysalises from my stems and gyrate inside,
come out with moist wings all discombobulat-
ed. Then they dry off and fuck off elsewhere
and sometimes I send one of my soft, seed
puffs after them, just because.

I am their food and their shelter. And you
idiots like to dig me up, poison me, replace
me with ornamental shrubbery. Keep it up
and I'll take every last one of those delicate
darlings down with me. No more monarchs
for you bastards. You'll get just white cabbage
moths. And you'll deserve them."

Cheatgrass

"Baby, here's the thing. I lay seed in any crack I can find. And sure, I care for you, but I can't have you losing your sheath every time I split a daisy cluster or pop sedum. Yeah, sedum are typically slutty but it ain't like you're keeping it in the *bromus tectorum* family.

This country was founded on principles of freedom, girl. We might be invasive, choking out the rights of the natives. But hell, I got to ramble. Anywhere I can get it and give it, honey.

It's why I got a taproot."

Violet

"Juggalos 4 Life."

Ground Ivy

"Pardon dear, but as you frolic, your skirt lifts and we are all eye-level with your nude ankles. Do not think me untoward in objecting to your mercurial nature, but you are coming off as an insensitive trollop.

Our young shan't suffer corruption by glimpsing your pale skin in such lascivious light. If they entertain notions of alternative lifestyles, of sexuality between what you call a man and a woman, they may shun our hermaphroditic pollen and the procreative succor it supplies.

Here, we have purchased you these *haute couture* stirrup pants and Body Glove water socks for the sake of our youth's developing sexuality."

Hairy Bittercress

"I know what you're thinking.

And yes, I keep it trimmed."

Mallow

"Remember when that sticky, white confection was made with the roots of my ancestors? The marshmallow was named after us. And humans had to seek out my kind and cultivate us, securing our lineage and our survival. Back before sugarcane got high and mighty and took over our role with their ability to make everything sweet and addictive. We were in your desserts and gelatin molds, sandwiched between chocolate and pastry crumble.

Now we are nothing more to you than ubiquitous trash with seed heads that look like little wheels of cheese. And that's *if* you notice us at all.

Back then, we were ballers. We balled so hard."

Broadleaf Plantain

"Crop? Oh, *that* kind of crop. I thought maybe you had one of those black, short whip things with you. But why would you carry one while out working the garden, sporting your wide-brimmed hat and your pink, rubber clogs?

Say, those shoes look pretty sturdy. If you happen to walk near me, I wouldn't mind if you took a few paces back and forth over my leaves. Press in with your heels a bit. I've been such a dirty plantain. Take out your anger on me for not being the other kind of plantain, the one you deep fry and serve with *frijoles* and *carne asada*.

Speaking of frying, if you have something hot and liquid, bring it outside and get rid of it. All over me, Mrs. Johnson."

Spurge

"My agent says I need to rebrand. I get mistaken for purslane, that bitch. Found a way to make waves among those raw food ninnies, she did.

True, I have red spots and milky sap. And sure, I'm not edible, but I do a great job of filling in cracks and empty spaces in soil. That has to count for something.

I'm thinking my tagline should be something like, *Splurge on Spurge* or *Spurge Me One More Time*. And for the logo, my flat leaves in grayscale, rambling over pavement, like a boss.

Then I can pen a missive on my new stationery, logo in the letterhead. It will begin with: *Fuck you, purslane, you degenerate waterweed.*"

Cannabis

THIS PAGE INTENTIONALLY LEFT BLANK.

CRABGRASS

"Calm yourself.

That is not leaf curl. Only peach trees and in-valids get leaf curl. You're fine! Except what's this crust on my leaf tips? I knew it! I knew I was dying. This will show them all for laughing at me for watching too much Dr. Oz. I bet it's scale. Heck, what's her name caught spider mites from that trashy arborvitae and no one thought that was possible. I'm going to die of leaf curl scale mites. New disease. I am the first disease vector.

If I must perish, I will take out every last pattypan squash plant in this yard. Sissies."

Chickweed

"Sure, I can understand your confusion. As hens, your brains are the size of what, cherry tomatoes?

But I've told you I am not cannabis. I have never even met cannabis. You never pull this crap with the henbit. Never try and get stoned off her leaves. What is it you guys need to escape from? Aside from pushing ovular worlds out of your pulsating cloaca everyday? Eggs bigger than your brains, heck, bigger than your heads?

Come to think of it, maybe you should get blitzed to beat the pain.

The morning glory is in the next plot over, FYI."

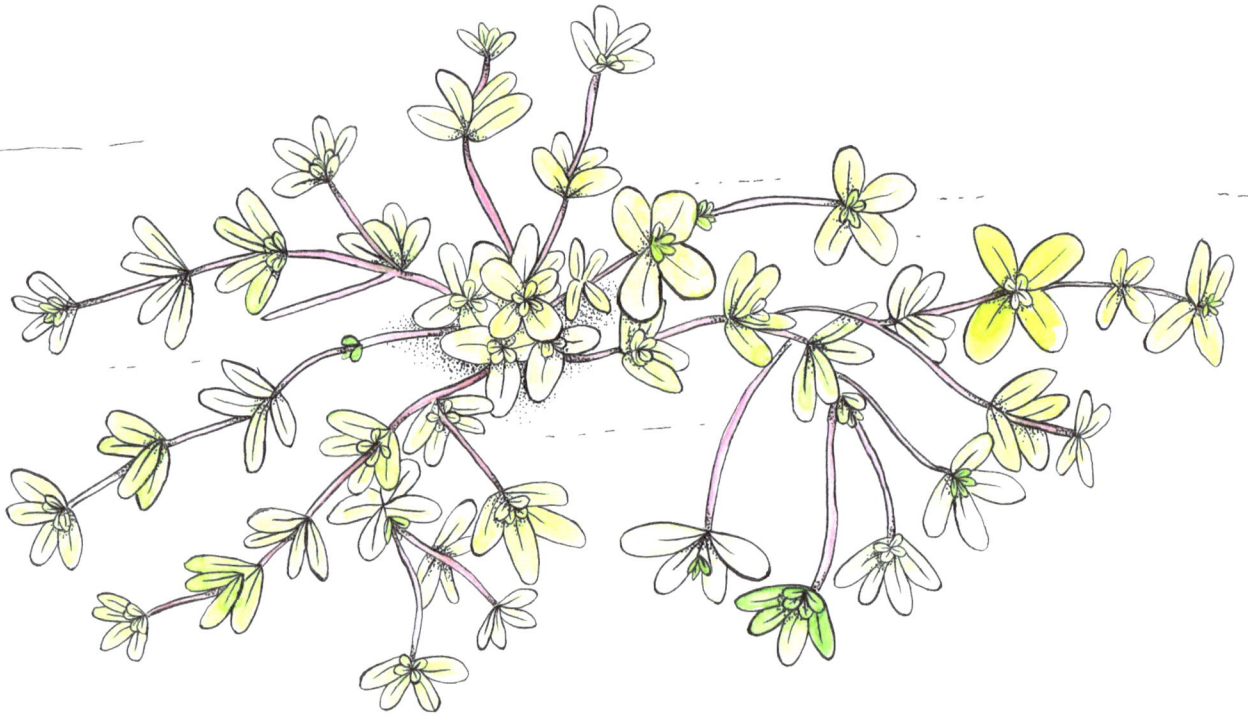

PURSLANE

"I never wanted this thug life.

It chose me. I've got the gray ash of tobacco leaves strewn at my base, Mountain Dew bottle caps keeping me company, a Powdered Donette wrapper as my only holmes.

In better circumstances, I could have ended up in someone's Greek salad, powering the souls attending a vegan potluck. Been a flower child who also happened to *be* a flower child.

But this compacted soil made me *hard*. I belong to the asphalt jungle. Mind helping me tip this 40 at my side? I'm feeling morose."

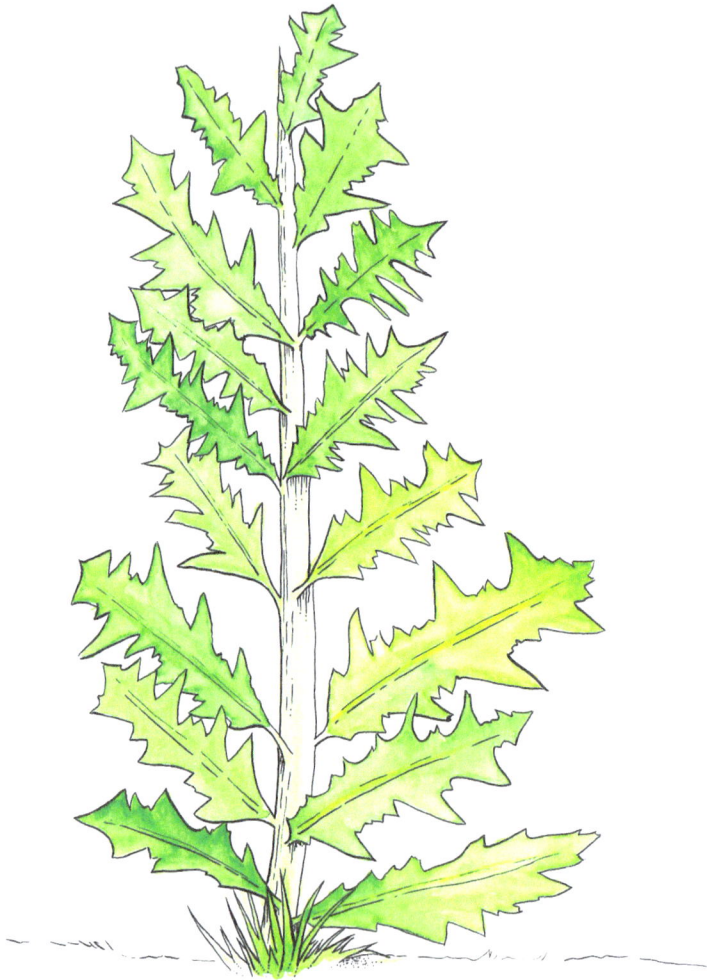

Prickly Lettuce

"Yesterday, the trowel came for Clarence.

I was hidden by a large maple leaf and spared the terror of cold metal sliding down my stem. But I saw the whole thing. He didn't scream. Well, he couldn't scream. But that's not the point. Clarence went with dignity.

Neither of us decided to seed down in the deep crack of this suburban driveway. We were blown here and grew here. It's our home, dammit. Yet we are hunted.

The trowel shall return. But I shall be waiting. My clear, stout spines shall prick through those cloth gloves and leave welts. Red splotches! And though I may perish, my white, stinging goo shall have satisfaction.

For me.

For Clarence.

My Clarence…"

Kudzu

"U LIKE STRANGLE??????

Sorry. Stuck on all CAPS. This texting thing is hard when my leaves can't type good. Let me try the voice recognition thing.

blank

Empty text bubble, right? I should try screaming into it.

blank

Brody, lay off, I AM talking into the mic.

blank

Well it SAYS it's an iPhone 7S. S stands for speaking. One more time.

blank

$%#@ this @*˄&er.

Fine. We can't call in a pro.

We'll have to just find something around us to asphyxiate, Brody."

Erica Crockett writes a lot. *What Weeds Are Thinking* is her first foray into the world of picture books. Her first novel, *Chemicals*, is about pharmaceuticals disappearing. Her other novels deal with serial killing, the stars, and Boise. Check out the first three books of *The Blood Zodiac*, starting with *The Ram*. Find her at www.ericacrockett.com.

An Idaho native, Sarah has been an artist all her life. She loves fantasy, webcomics, gardening, and a really good chocolate stout. Sarah can be found on Instagram @serocreates or Twitter @sarahlzrblaster.

Books by Erica Crockett

Available Now!

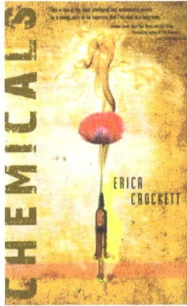

CHEMICALS: When America is forced to deal with the fallout of its War on Drugs, the country is left without access to the pharmaceuticals it depends on for survival. A group held together by a woman with a martyr complex tries to stay alive and avoid the allure of illicit drugs, crime, and chaos.

THE RAM: CYCLE 1 of THE BLOOD ZODIAC: Peach Barrow is desperate to change the course of her life; she's willing to do anything to become a woman of power, spirit and control. Riley Wanner is just trying to keep his life together. After an accident leaves him doubting his career, relationships with women and his addictions, he's uncertain where to turn next. Both of them narrow in on a stripper at a local club. And their attention spirals into events tainted with ritual, violence, sex and conquest.

www.ingramcontent.com/pod-product-compliance
Lightning Source LLC
LaVergne TN
LVHW072053070426
835508LV00002B/80